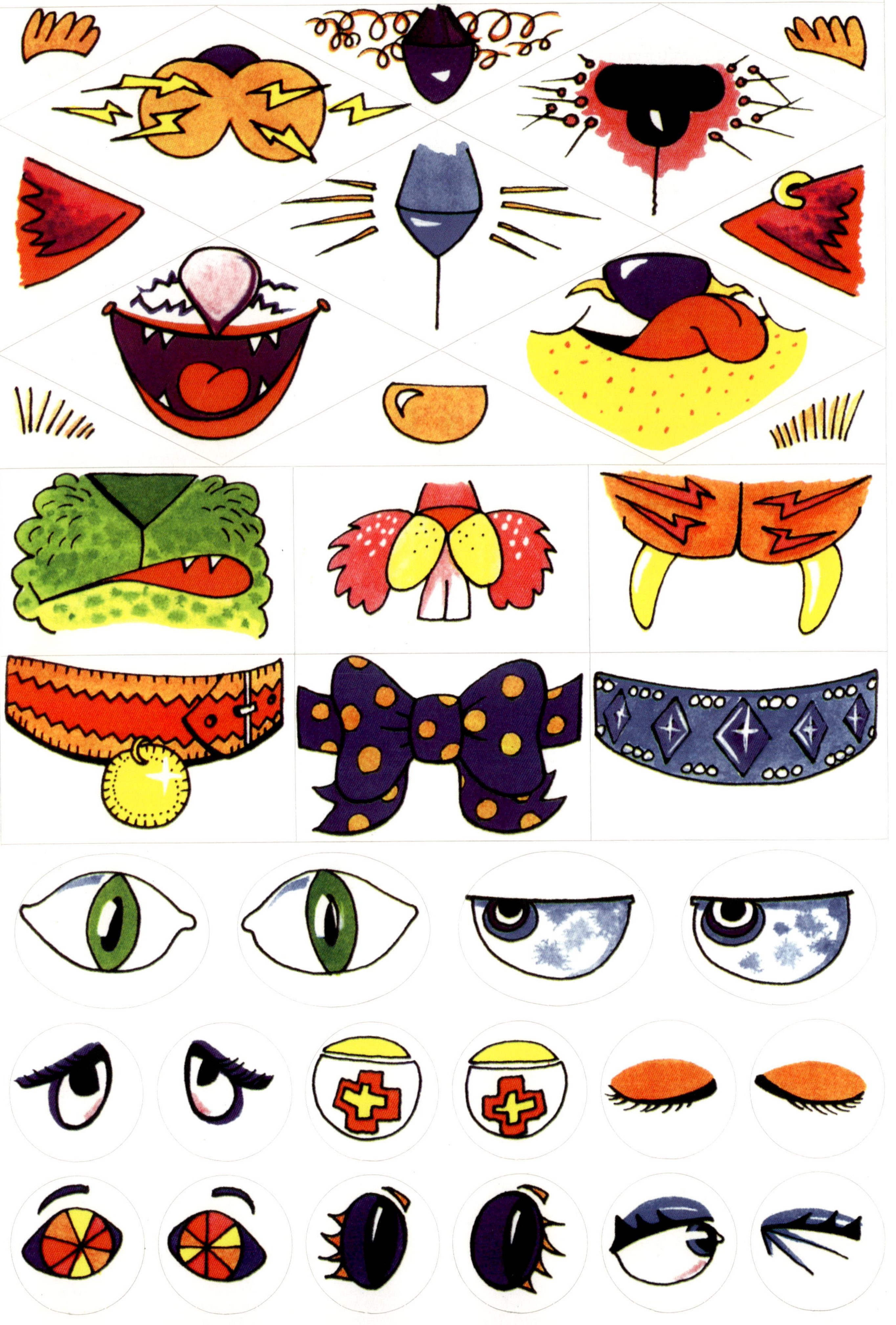

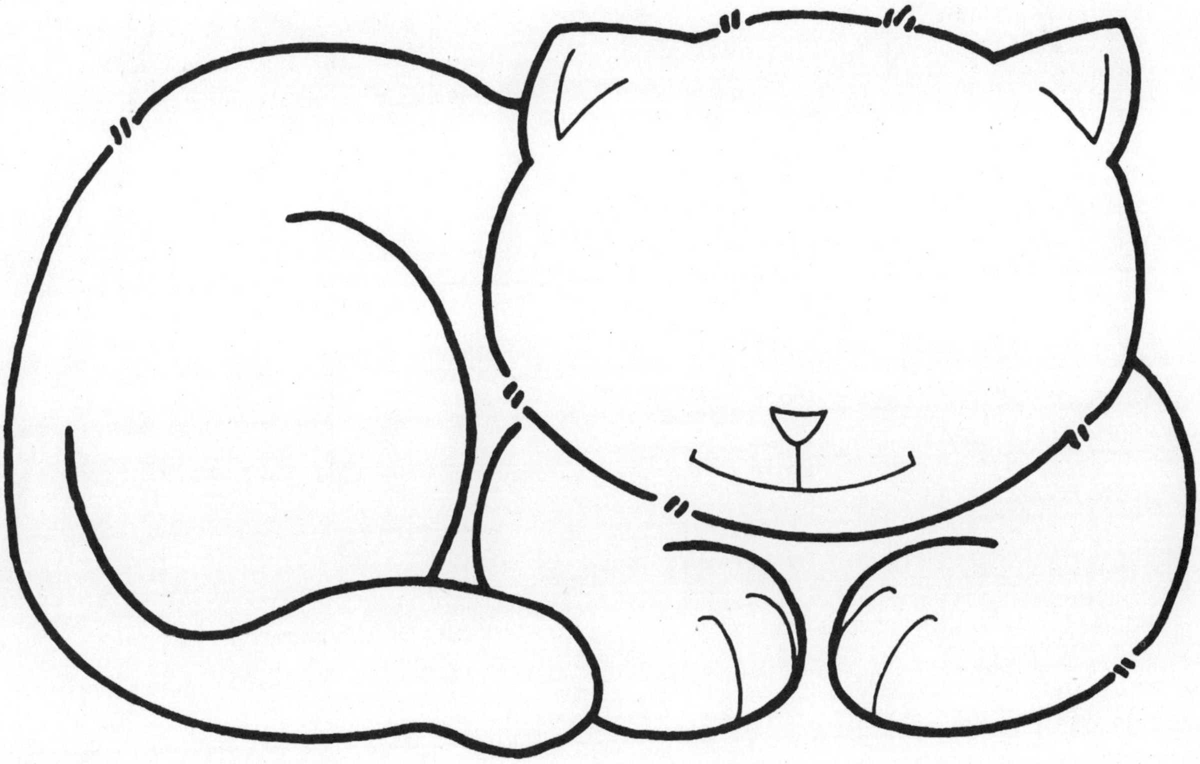

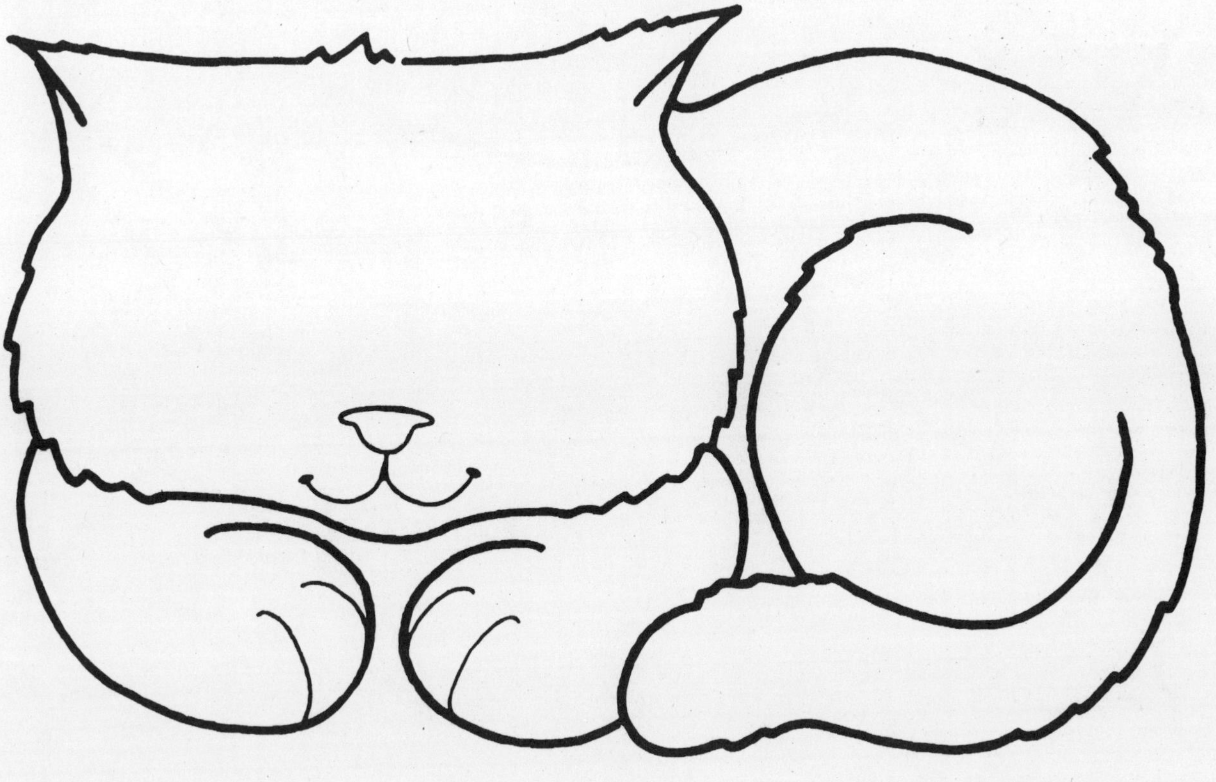

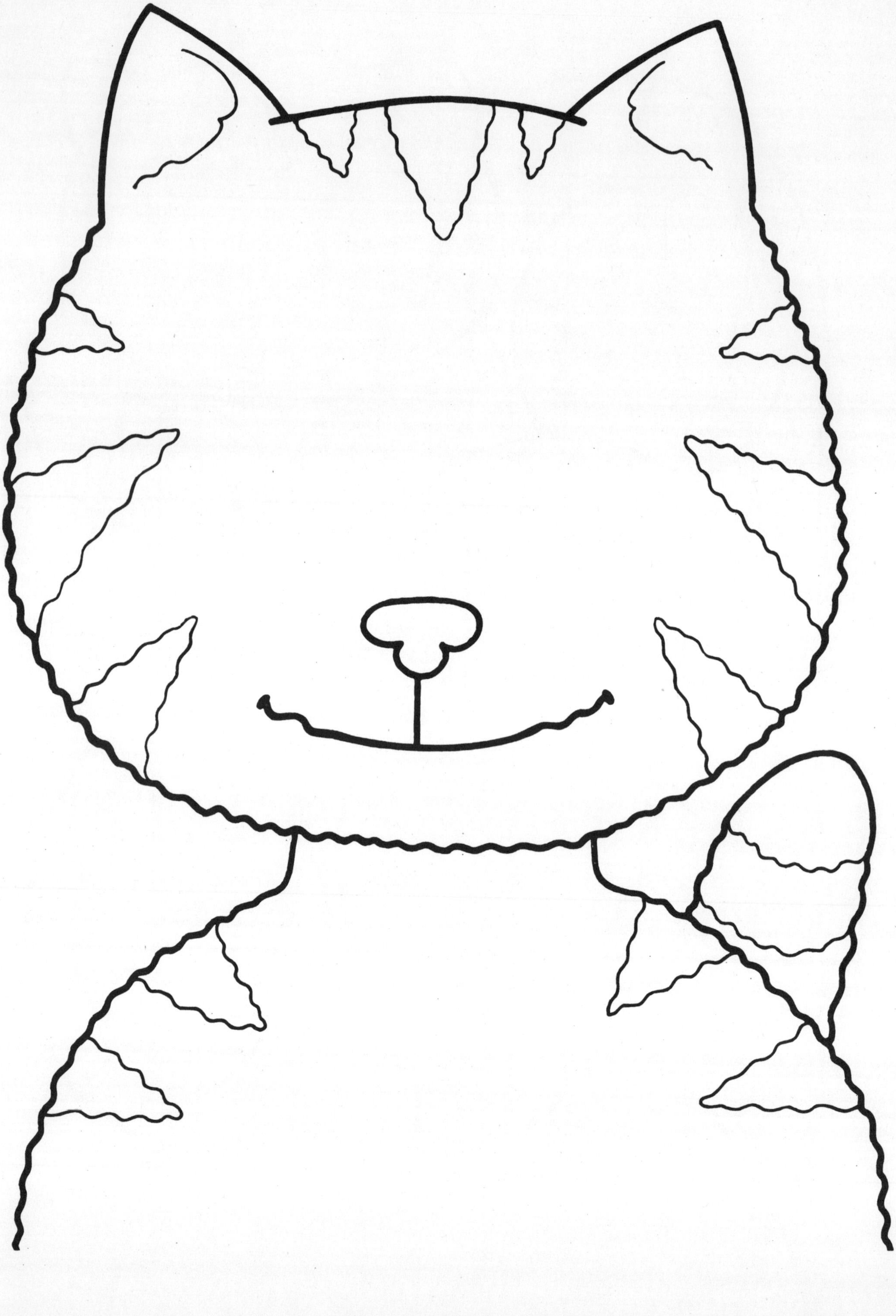

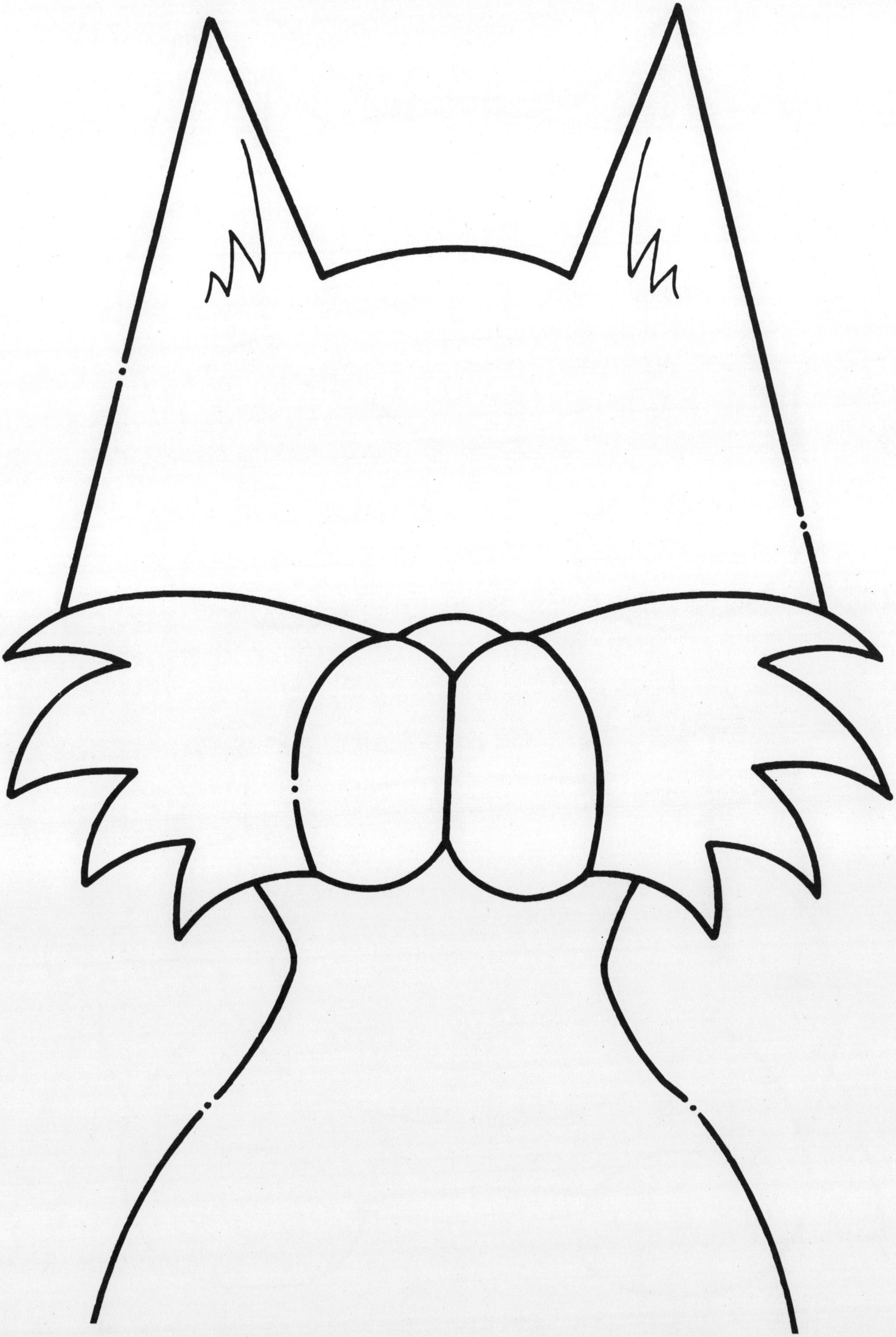

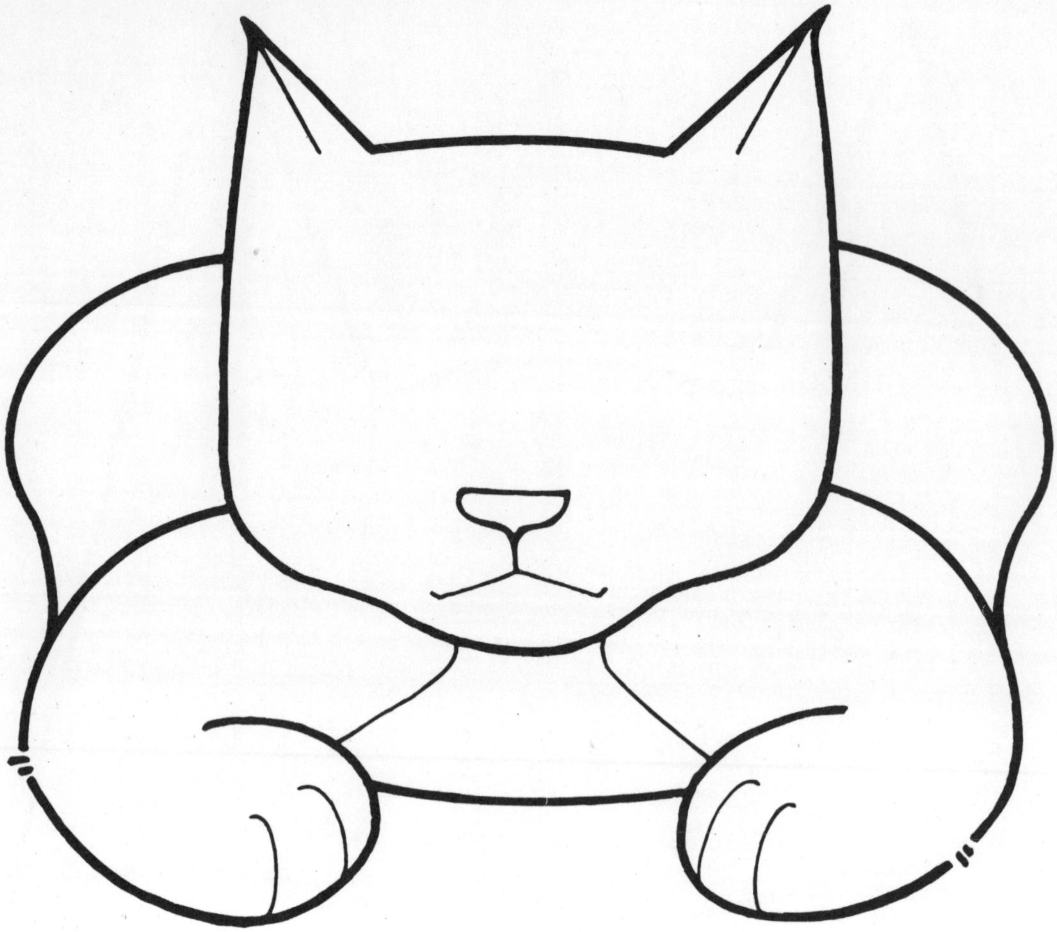

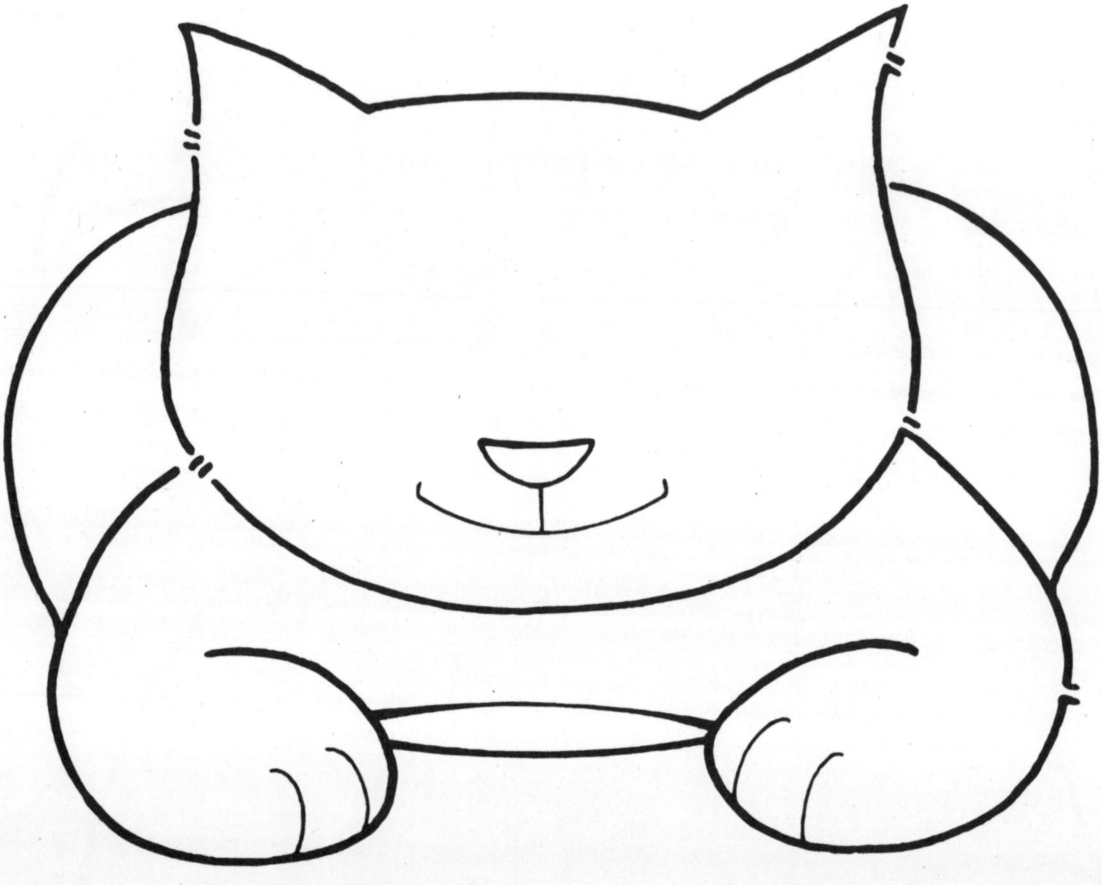

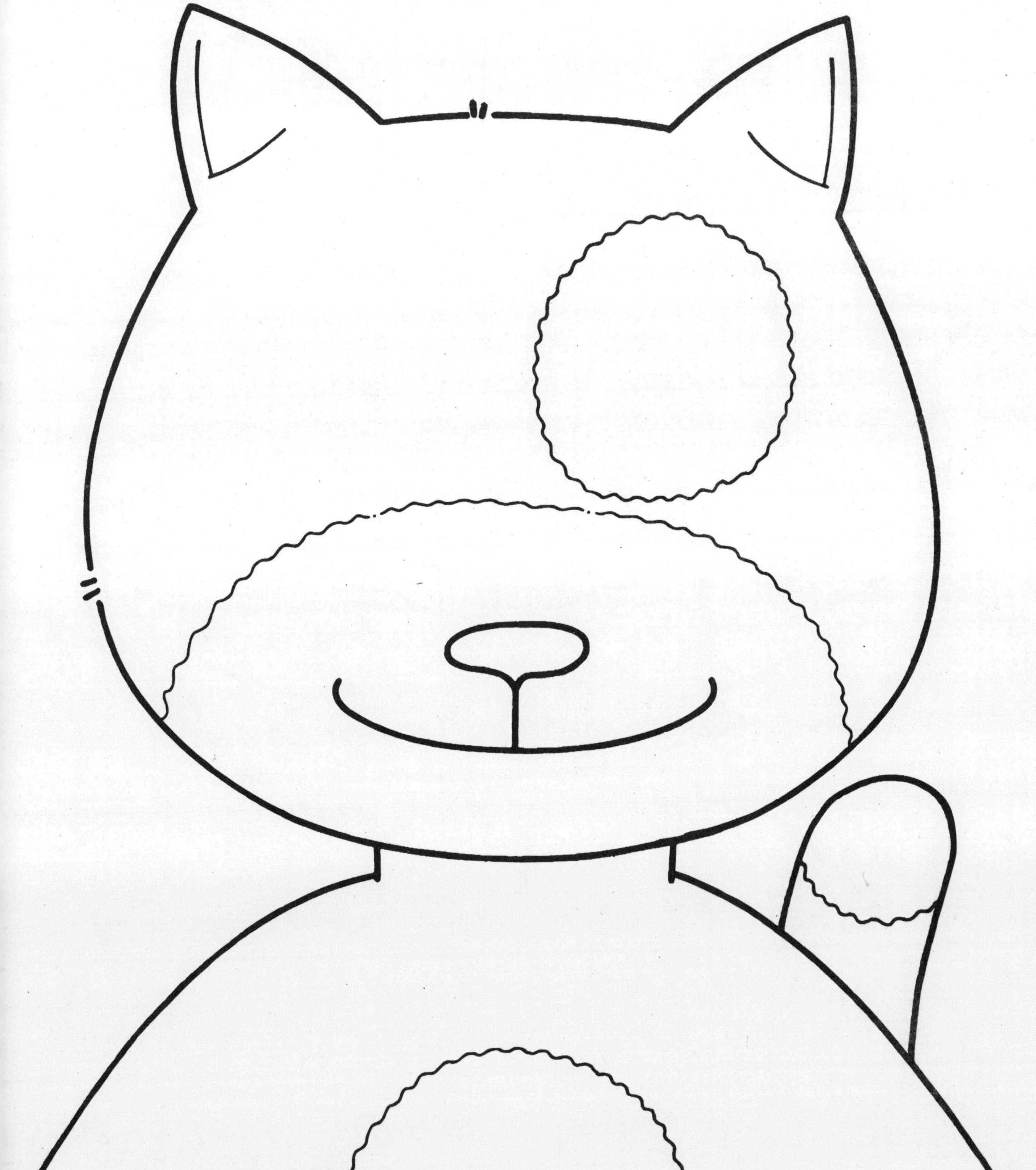

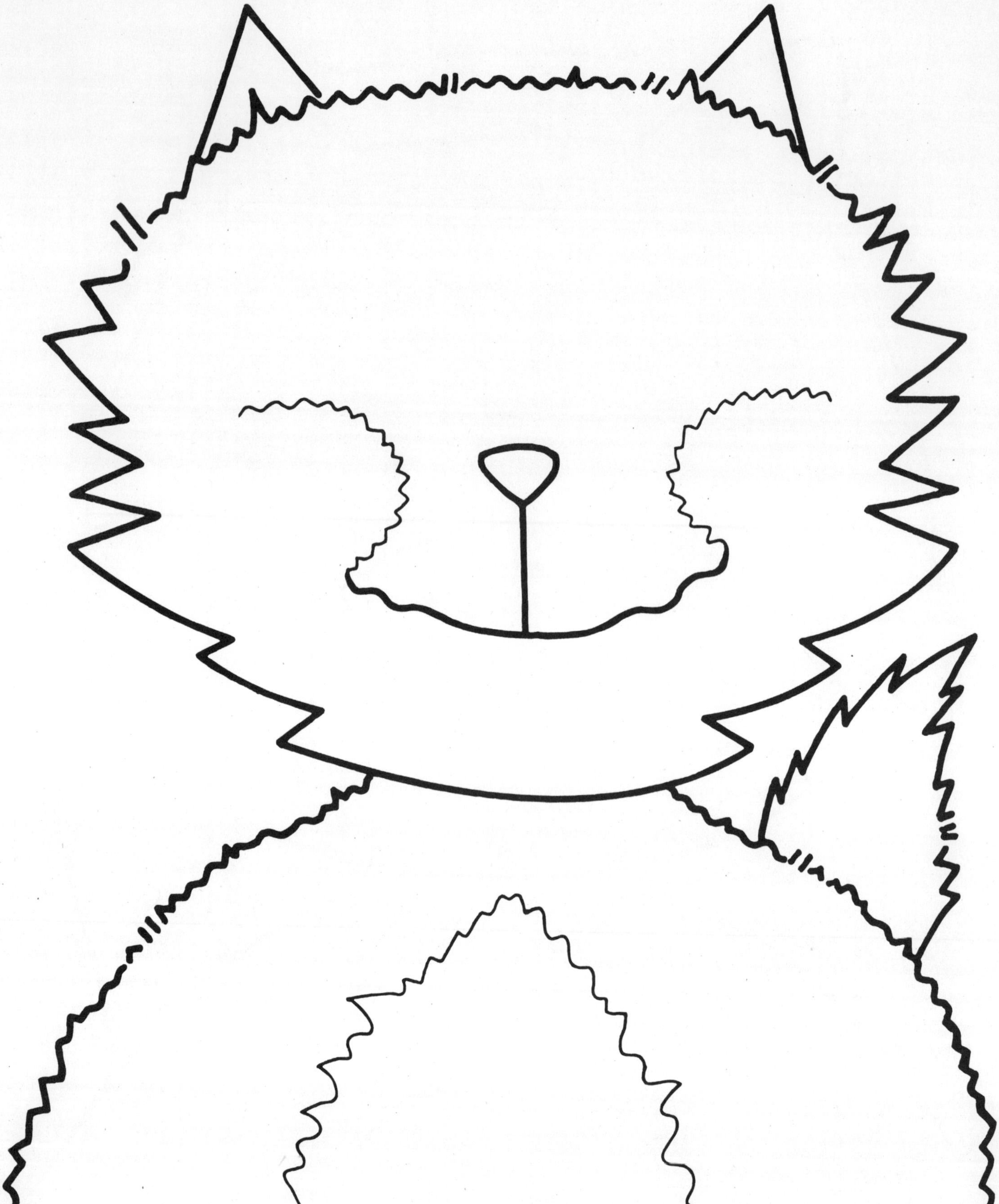

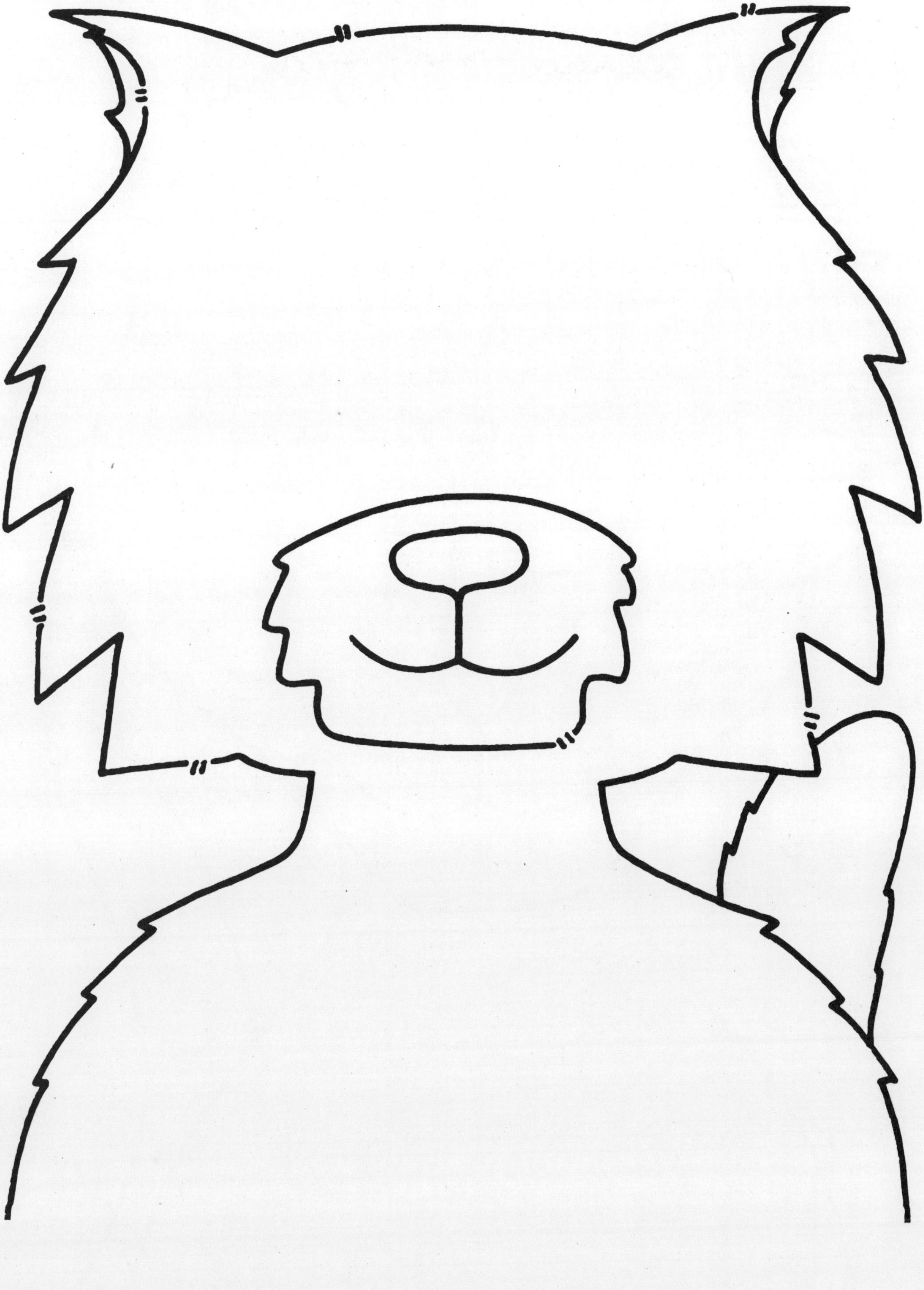

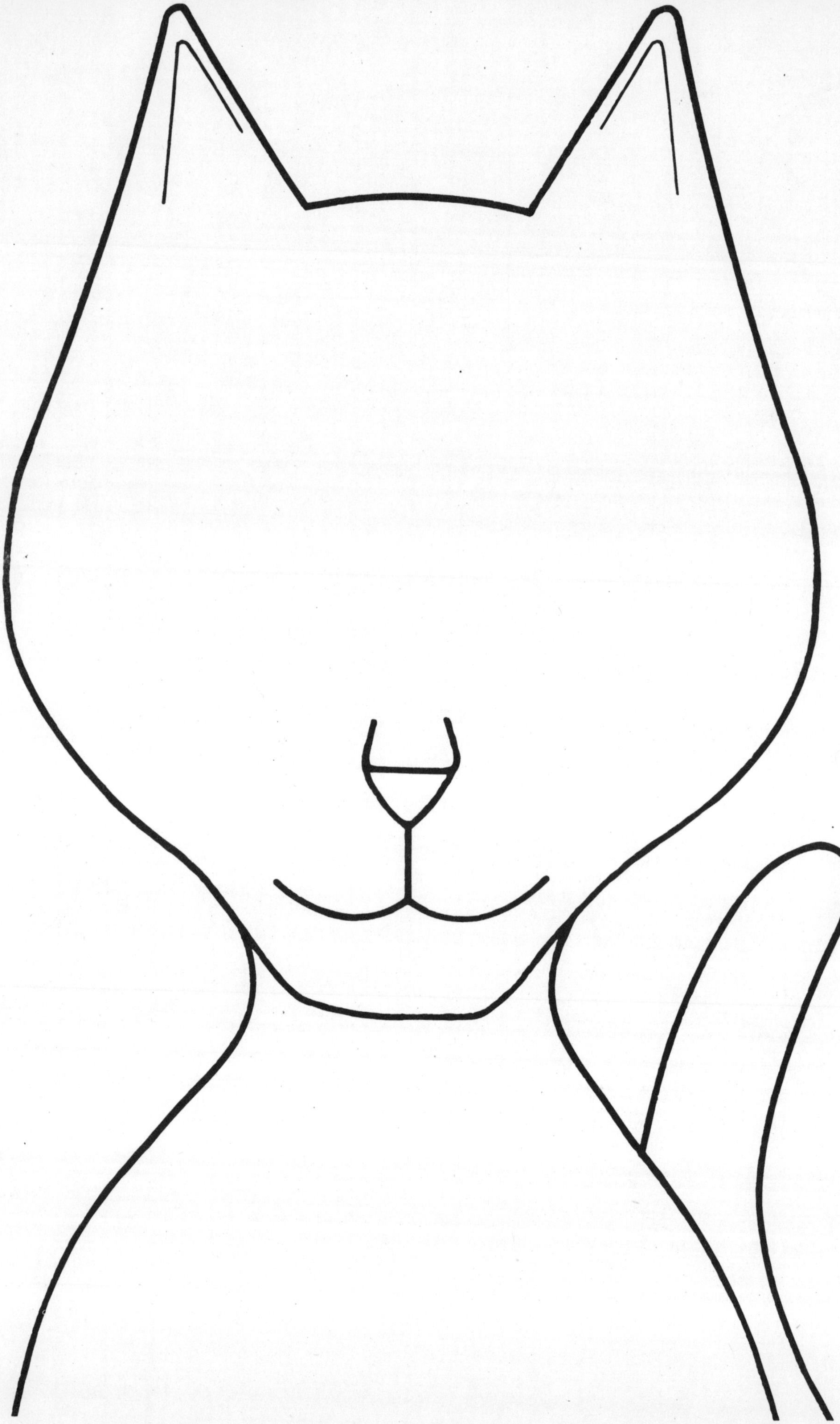

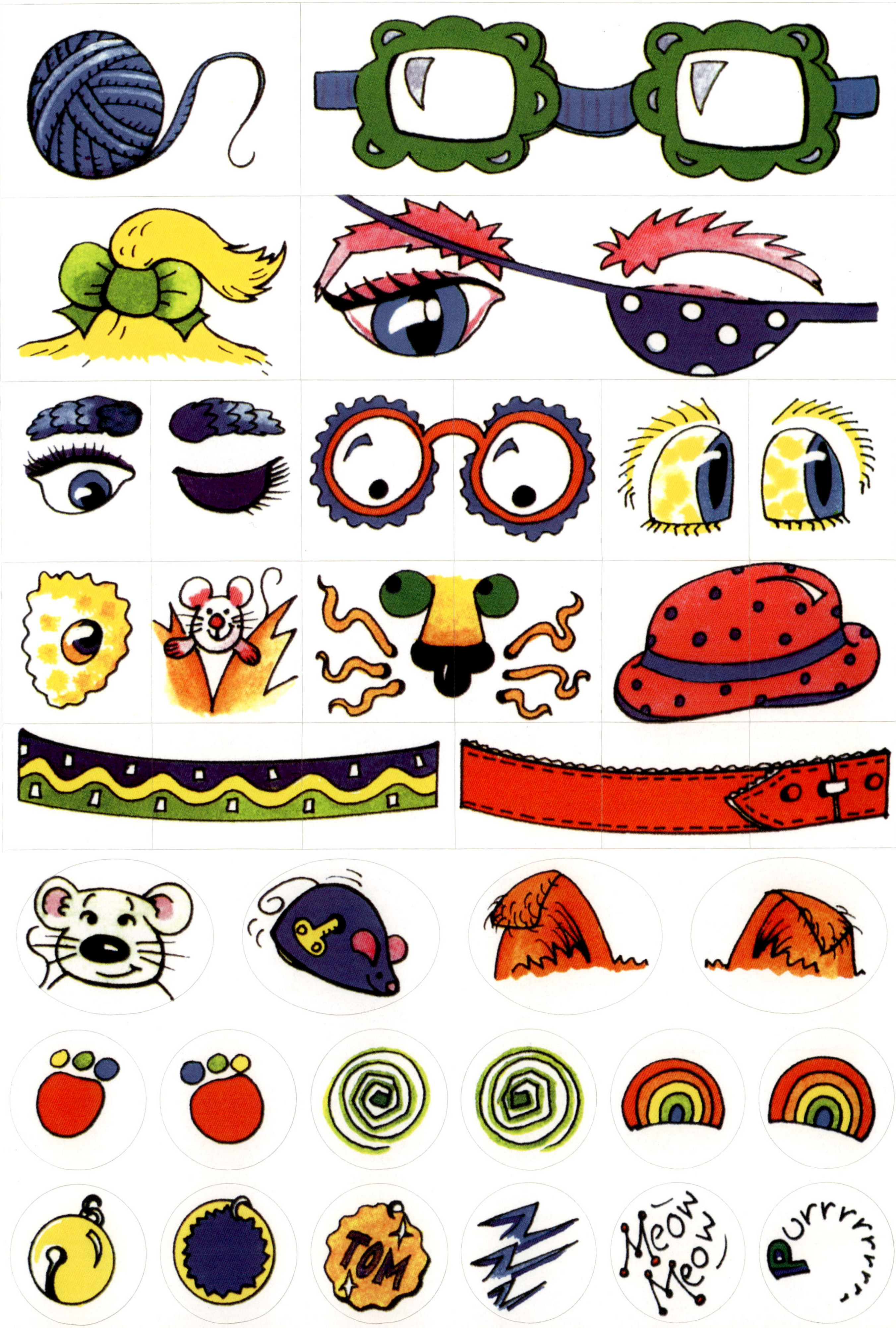
TOM
Meow
Meow
Purrrrrrr